LANGUAGE ARTS

Learning About

Folktales, Fables, and Fairy Tales

by Martha E. H. Rustad

Consulting Editor: Gail Saunders-Smith, PhD
Consultant: Kelly Boswell, educational consultant

CAPSTONE PRESS
a capstone imprint

Pebble Plus is published by Capstone Press,
1710 Roe Crest Drive, North Mankato, Minnesota 56003
www.capstonepub.com

Library of Congress Cataloging-in-Publication Data
Rustad, Martha E. H. (Martha Elizabeth Hillman), 1975–
    Learning about folktales, fables, and fairy tales / Martha E. H. Rustad.
        pages cm.— (Language arts)
    Includes bibliographical references and index.
    ISBN 978-1-4914-0577-2 (hb)—ISBN 978-1-4914-0611-3 (eb)—ISBN 978-1-4914-0645-8 (pb)
    1. Folklore—Juvenile literature. 2. Authorship—Juvenile literature. 3. Storytelling—Juvenile literature. I. Title.
    GR74R87 2015
    398.2—dc23   2014001854

Editorial Credits
Erika L. Shores, editor; Terri Poburka, designer; Charmaine Whitman, production specialist

Photo Credits
Capstone Studio: Karon Dubke, 7; Corbis: Blue Lantern Studio, 11, Christie's Images, 21; Getty Images: LCDM Unversal History Archive, 13; Mary Evans Picture Library: Peter & Dawn Cope Collection, 17; Newscom: akg-images, 9; Robana via Getty Images: The British Library, 15; Shutterstock: John A Davis, 19, lanych, cover (girl), Matthew Cole, cover (castle); UIG via Getty Images: Universal History Archive, 5

For Melissa.—MEHR

Note to Parents and Teachers

The Language Arts set supports Common Core State Standards for Language Arts related to craft and structure, to text types and writing purpose, and to research for building and presenting knowledge. This book describes and illustrates folktales, fairy tales, and fables. The images support early readers in understanding the text. The repetition of words and phrases helps early readers learn new words. This book also introduces early readers to subject-specific vocabulary words, which are defined in the Glossary section. Early readers may need assistance to read some words and to use the Table of Contents, Glossary, Read More, Internet Sites, Critical Thinking Using the Common Core, and Index sections of the book.

Printed in the United States of America in North Mankato, Minnesota.
032014   008087CGF14

Table of Contents

Once Upon a Time 4
Setting and Characters . . . 8
Kinds of Folklore 12
Beginnings and Endings . . . 18

Glossary 22
Read More 23
Internet Sites 23
Critical Thinking Using
the Common Core 24
Index 24

Once Upon a Time

Tell me a story! Folklore is

made up of stories from long ago.

People told them over and over.

These folktales, fables, and

fairy tales were told out loud.

Most folktales, fables, and
fairy tales do not have an author.
No one knows who first told
the story. Writers gather them
into books.

Setting and Characters

The setting is when and where a story takes place. Folktales, fables, and fairy tales often take place in faraway lands. Storytellers say they happened long ago.

from "Hansel and Gretel"

Once upon a time, a brother and sister were lost in the woods. They came upon a house made of candy. The sister broke off a piece and began to eat.

"Brother," Gretel said. "This tastes so good!"

"I'll try just a bit," Hansel said.

Suddenly a wicked witch appeared. "Who is nibbling on my house!" cried the witch.

Sometimes odd characters are in these stories. Animals talk. Kids meet trolls. Giants roam.

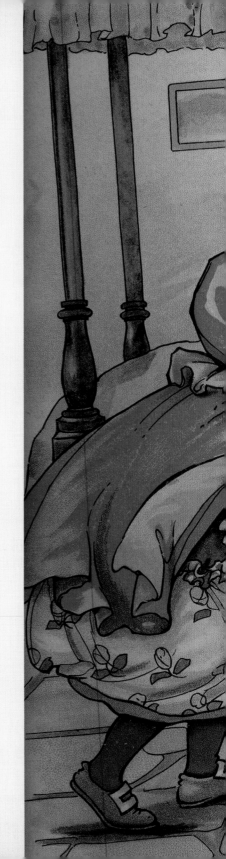

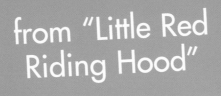

The wolf dressed in grandmother's clothes, and climbed into her bed.

Little Red Riding Hood knocked on the door.

"Come in!" said the wolf.

Little Red Riding Hood said, "Grandmother, your voice sounds scratchy!"

"Oh, that is just my sore throat," said the wolf.

"My, what big eyes you have!" Little Red Riding Hood exclaimed.

"The better to see you with, my dear," said the wolf.

Kinds of Folklore

Tall tales are stories that are a part of folklore. These exciting tales might explain something. One tall tale tells how a giant made Minnesota's lakes.

from "Paul Bunyan and Babe the Blue Ox"

One day Paul Bunyan and Babe the Blue Ox played a game of tag. They ran around, each trying to catch the other. When they stopped to rest, they looked at the many footprints they had left behind. Rain began to fall and filled up their huge footprints. And that's how Minnesota's 10,000 lakes were made.

In fables, animals often
learn lessons. In one fable,
a grasshopper learns to work
before he plays.

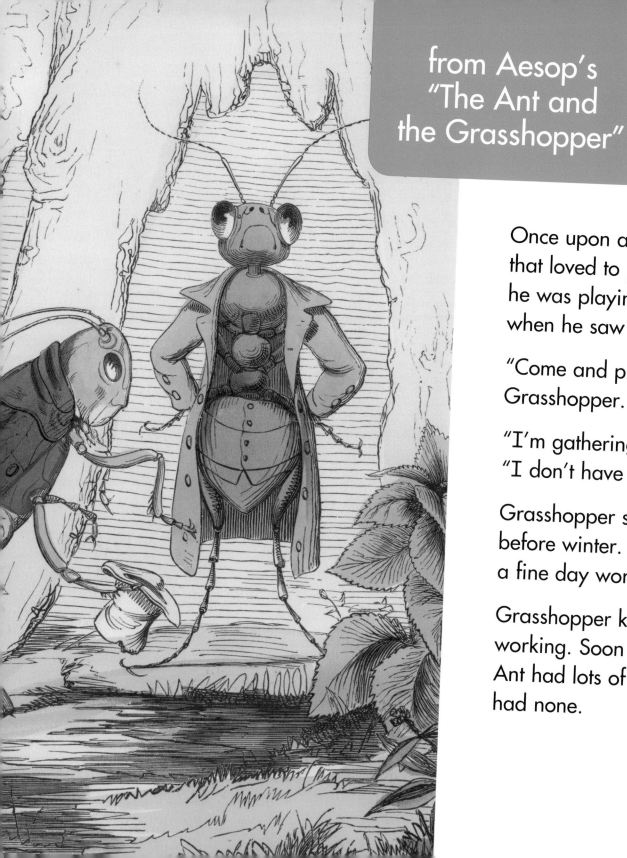

Once upon a time, there was a grasshopper that loved to play all day. One fall day, he was playing in a pile of leaves when he saw an ant working hard.

"Come and play with me, Ant," said Grasshopper. "It's a beautiful day to play."

"I'm gathering food for winter," replied Ant. "I don't have time to play now."

Grasshopper said, "There is plenty of time before winter. I'm not going to waste such a fine day working."

Grasshopper kept playing, while Ant kept working. Soon the snow began to fly. Ant had lots of food, but Grasshopper had none.

In fairy tales, some problems are solved using magic. Characters meet magical witches, giants, and fairies. The story changes in different countries.

from "Cinderella,"
story from France

As Cinderella hurried away from the ball, she dropped a glass slipper from her fairy godmother. The prince found the tiny shoe. He asked every girl in the kingdom to try it on. The slipper was much too small for everyone—except Cinderella.

from "Ye Xian"
(YEE SHEN),
story from China

As Ye Xian left the festival, she left behind one of her golden shoes from the magic fish. The king wanted to find the girl who wore it. He put it on display, and every girl tried it on. It fit no one. The guards caught Ye Xian trying on the shoe. They thought she was trying to steal it. But the shoe fit her tiny foot perfectly.

Beginnings and Endings

Folklore stories begin "Once upon a time." Different cultures begin stories with different words. This one starts "Long ago when the world was young."

from the Cherokee Indian story "How the Milky Way Came to Be"

Long ago when the world was young, there were not many stars in the sky. The people needed cornmeal to live. One night a dog stole a bag of cornmeal. The people chased him away. As he ran, he spilled the cornmeal across the sky. The grains of cornmeal turned into stars.

Stories often end with the same words. Some end with, "And they lived happily ever after."

This story ends with "Snip, snap, snout! This tale's told out."

from "The Three Billy Goats Gruff"

The biggest billy goat Gruff joined his brothers on the hill. They ate and ate and ate, and grew fat. And as far as I know, they are still there today.

Snip, snap, snout! This tale's told out.

Glossary

author—someone who writes books

character—a person or animal in a story

culture—the way of life, customs, ideas, and traditions of a group of people

fable—a story that teaches moral lessons; fables often feature talking animals

fairy tale—a story about magic creatures in an imaginary place

folklore—tales, sayings, and customs among a group of people

folktale—a story told out loud by many people

tall tale—an exciting story about events that are often made up

setting—the place and time of a story

Read More

Alexander, Carol. *How to Tell a Folktale.* Text Styles. New York: Crabtree Pub. Co., 2012.

Pullman, Philip, ed. *Fairy Tales from the Brothers Grimm: A New English Version.* New York: Viking, 2012.

Shaskan, Trisha Speed. *Honestly, Red Riding Hood Was Rotten!: The Story of Little Red Riding Hood as Told by the Wolf.* Mankato, Minn.: Picture Window Books, 2012.

Internet Sites

FactHound offers a safe, fun way to find Internet sites related to this book. All of the sites on FactHound have been researched by our staff.

Here's all you do:

Visit *www.facthound.com*

Type in this code: 9781491405772

Super-cool stuff!

Check out projects, games and lots more at
www.capstonekids.com

Critical Thinking Using the Common Core

1. Look at the illustration on page 11. Describe who the main characters are in this fairy tale. (Key Ideas and Details)

2. On page 17 two different versions of the Cinderella fairy tale are told. Describe some of the ways in which the stories differ. (Key Ideas and Details)

Index

"The Ant and the
   Grasshopper," 15
authors, 6
beginnings, 18
books, 6
characters, 10, 16
"Cinderella," 17
endings, 20
fables, 4, 6, 8, 14
fairy tales, 4, 6, 8, 16
faraway lands, 8
folktales, 4, 6, 8

"Hansel and Gretel," 9
"How the Milky Way
   Came to Be," 19
lessons, 14
"Little Red Riding Hood," 11
magic, 16
"Paul Bunyan and Babe
   the Blue Ox," 13
settings, 8
tall tales, 12
"The Three Billy Goats
   Gruff," 21

Word Count: 210 (main text)
Grade: 1
Early-Intervention Level: 22